THE NARADA WILDERNESS COLLECTION

TABLE OF CONTENTS

Hal Leonard Publishing Corporation
7777 West Bluemound Road P.O. Box 13819 Milwaukee, WI 53213

INTRODUCTION

Climb the mountains and get their good tidings;
Nature's peace will flow into you as sunshine
into flowers; the winds will blow their freshness
into you and the storms their energy, and cares
will drop off like autumn leaves.

— John Muir

THE NARADA WILDERNESS COLLECTION was created as a celebration of our cherished wilderness lands — lands that provide all of us with a priceless refuge from the symmetry and efficiency of our urbanized world, a haven for our creative instincts, a sanctuary for the renewal of the human spirit.

Narada is donating a portion of the proceeds from the recording to three major wilderness defenders — the National Audubon Society, the Sierra Club and The Wilderness Society. Together, we hope that our society's appreciation for these irreplaceable natural treasures will continue to grow, ensuring that future generations may be forever refreshed by what John Muir described as "the tonic of wilderness."

ISBN 0-7935-1215-8

Cover image by Greg Ryan
Design by Connie Gage, Frank Gosein, Eric Lindert and John Morey

© 1992 Nara Music, Inc. and Amida Music, Inc.
1845 N. Farwell Avenue, Milwaukee, WI 53202 USA
Tel. 414-272-6700

NP-90002SB

BREAK OF DAY

My song describes the first light of day in the wilderness, and the joy that comes from the alchemy of the earth, the sun and the people. The wind instruments represent the wind in the mountains, the flute invokes the arrival of sunlight, the percussion is the heartbeat of the earth, the synthesizers color the sky, the charango is the life of the earth — the birds, the animals, the plants — and the melody is the people, at first calling to each other, then celebrating in a dance.

By BERNARDO RUBAJA

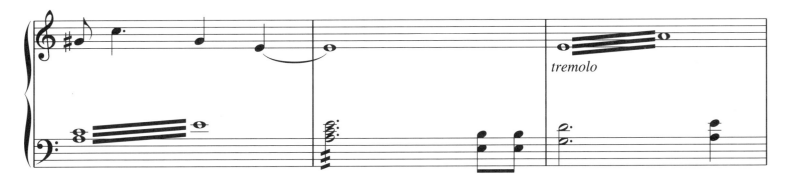

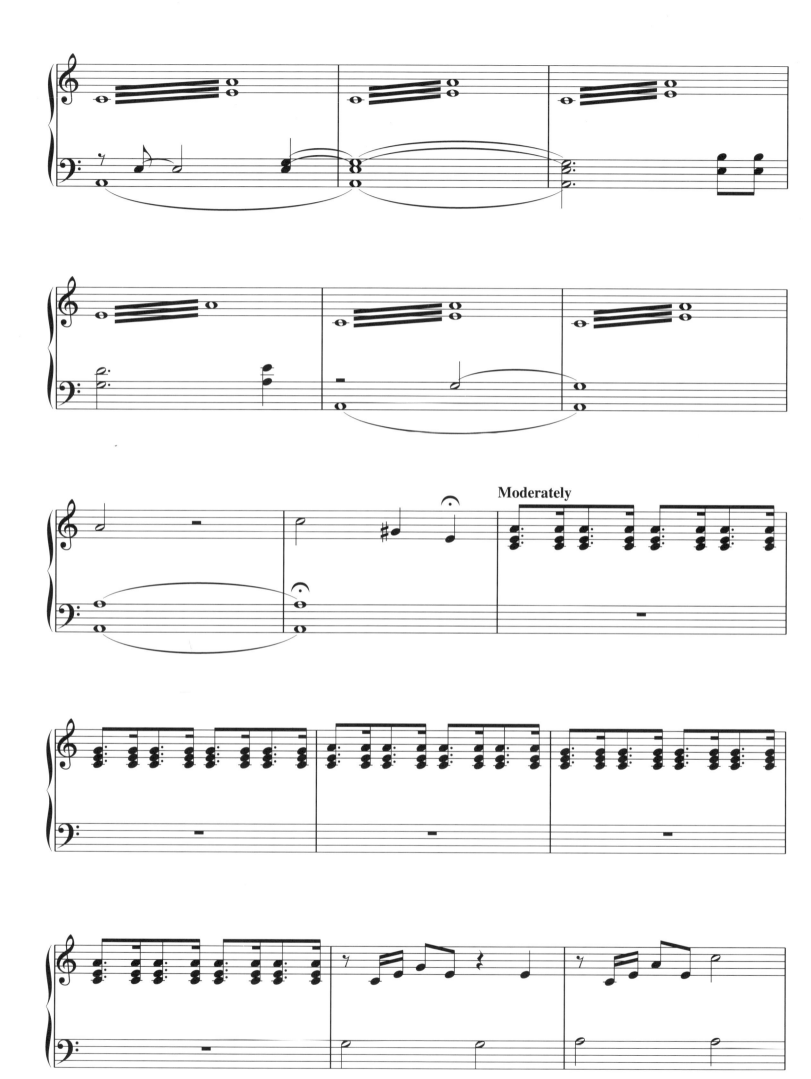

To Coda ⊕

D.S. al Coda

CODA

SAHARA SUNRISE

I have visited more than 40 countries during my travels, and of all the landscapes I have observed, none fascinates me more than the desert. In the area south of Morocco, the Sahara Desert is remarkable to see. It is so very clean, so quiet, so empty of people — nothing but a world of gold, gray and  *blue. The desert is a place of extremes and harsh contrasts, but it is also a place that offers us a special kind of beauty and drama found nowhere else in nature.*

By RALF ILLENBERGER

Moderately bright

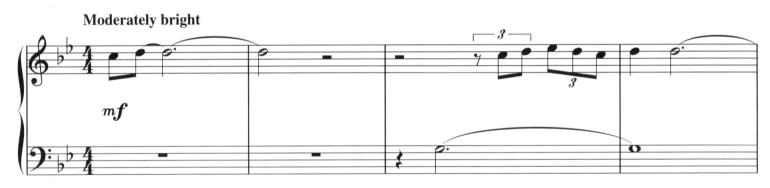

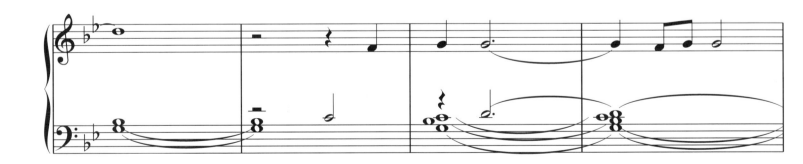

11

EARLY MOON AND FIRELIGHT

In special places of the northeastern United States — from Maine to the central lakes of New Hampshire to the magical, lake-filled forests of the Adirondacks — nature's haunting beauty is most powerfully evoked by the soulful echoes of the loons. Their cries are the music of the lake and the starry northern sky. Don't go there with a plan — you are part of the sanctuary of nature, and your company is the trees and the wind. Just go, listen to your heart, and bring back what you find.

Dedicated to Dean Rhoads

Artist portrait by Richard Anderson

By CAROL NETHEN

Slowly and Freely

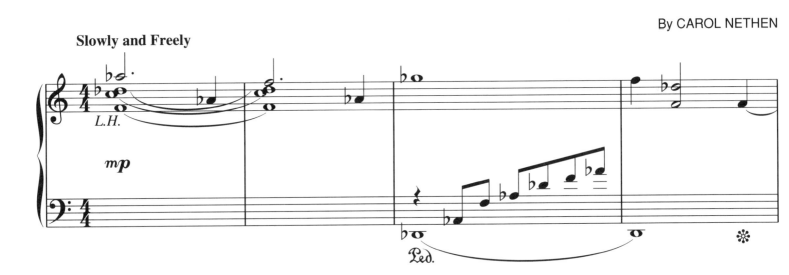

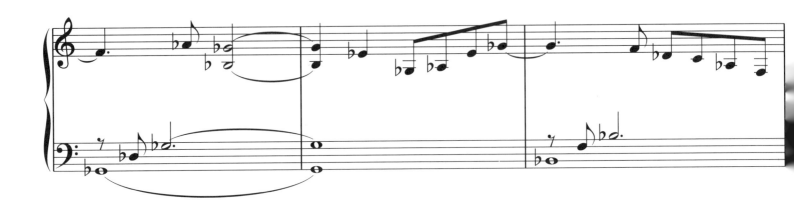

© 1990 Amida Music, Inc.
1845 North Farwell Avenue, Milwaukee, WI 53202

FRAGILE MAJESTY

The Wilderness Act of 1964. The Clean Air Act of 1970. The Endangered Species Act of 1973. Future generations may some day regard environmental legislation of the late 20th century with the same significance that we today attribute to the Magna Carta or the Bill of Rights. To us, preserving our

wilderness lands and forests is as well-being. Nature appears so too often take it for granted. We are not only its beauty, but also its

important as ensuring our personal powerful and enduring that people all obligated, though, to appreciate preciousness and fragility.

Artist portrait by Mark Gubin

By ERIC TINGSTAD
and NANCY RUMBEL

Gently flowing (♩ = 116)

mf

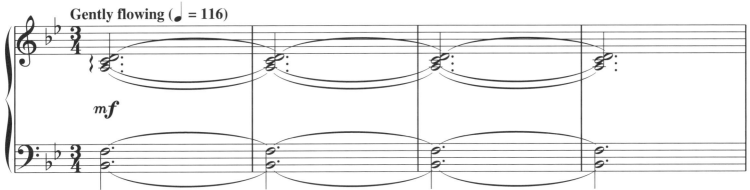

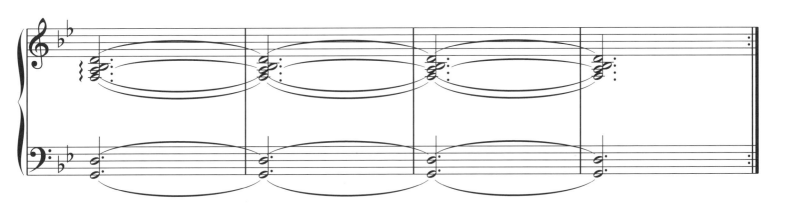

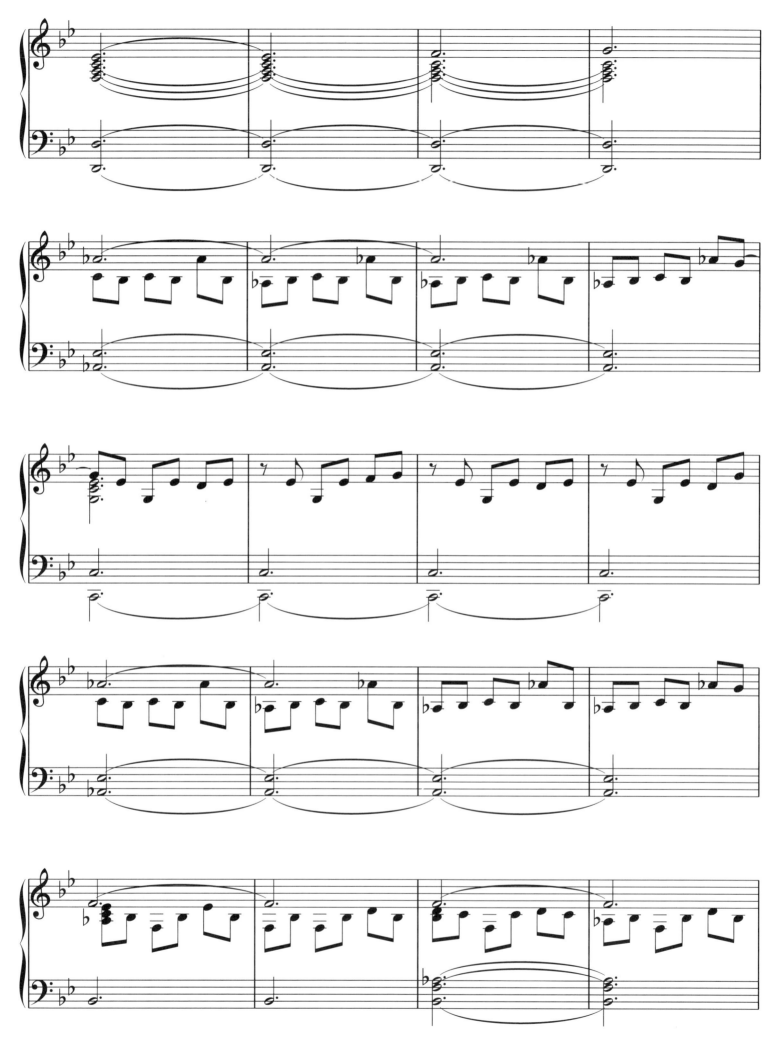

To Coda ⊕

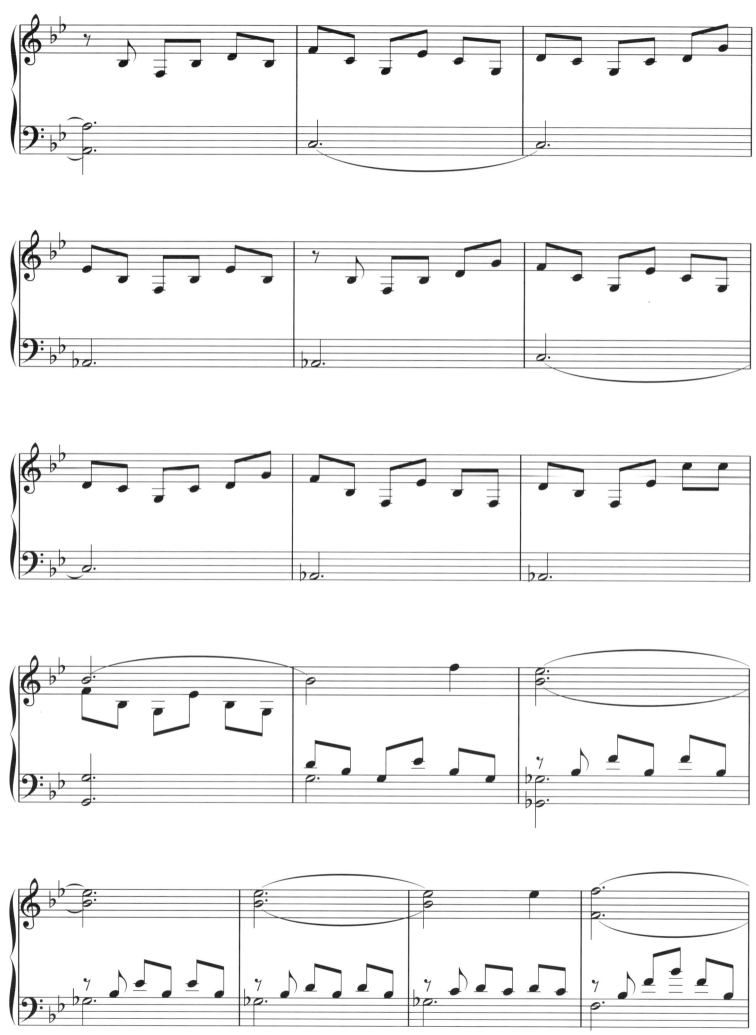

MADRE DE LA TIERRA

To help commemorate the 20th anniversary of Earth Day, a Public Broadcasting affiliate asked me to write a special composition. The title of the piece means "mother of the land," and its meaning can be viewed two ways. First, we need to appreciate all that Mother

Nature — the spirit of nature, the now, even more importantly, we protective attributes. Mom's not to show her care, respect and

spirit of life — has given us, and need to acquire her motherly, feeling so well, and she needs us gentleness.

Artist portrait by Davis Freeman

By DAVID LANZ

8va bassa

NORTHERN MORNING

When you wake up next to a lake, or beneath a thick canopy of towering Douglas fir, or on the floor of an expansive valley, you begin the day with a renewed frame of mind, an outlook that too often eludes you when you wake up surrounded by steel, glass and concrete. I'm beginning to sense that our society, at long last, is waking up with a new perspective on wilderness lands. People are beginning to comprehend the pricelessness of open, wild areas, recognizing that the greatest resource they offer us is not their timber or minerals, but their life-affirming intangibles.

By PETER BUFFETT

Moderately

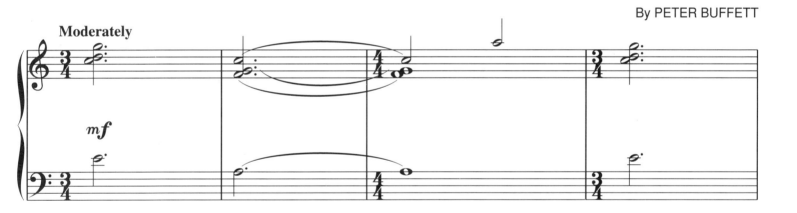

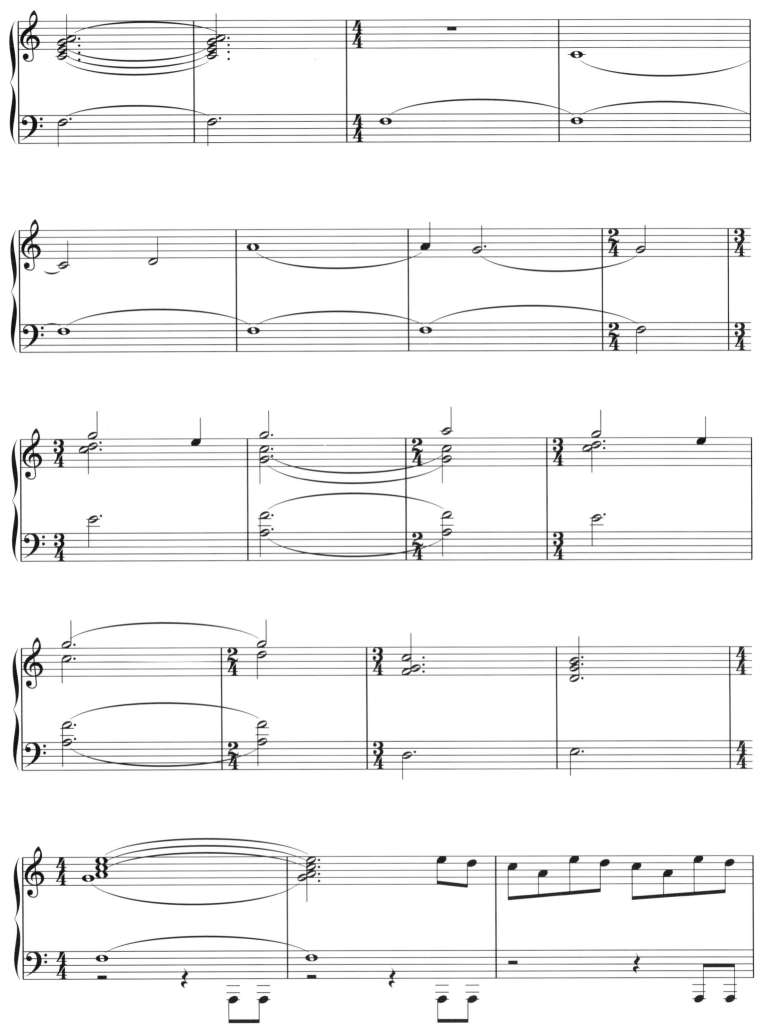

Tempo I

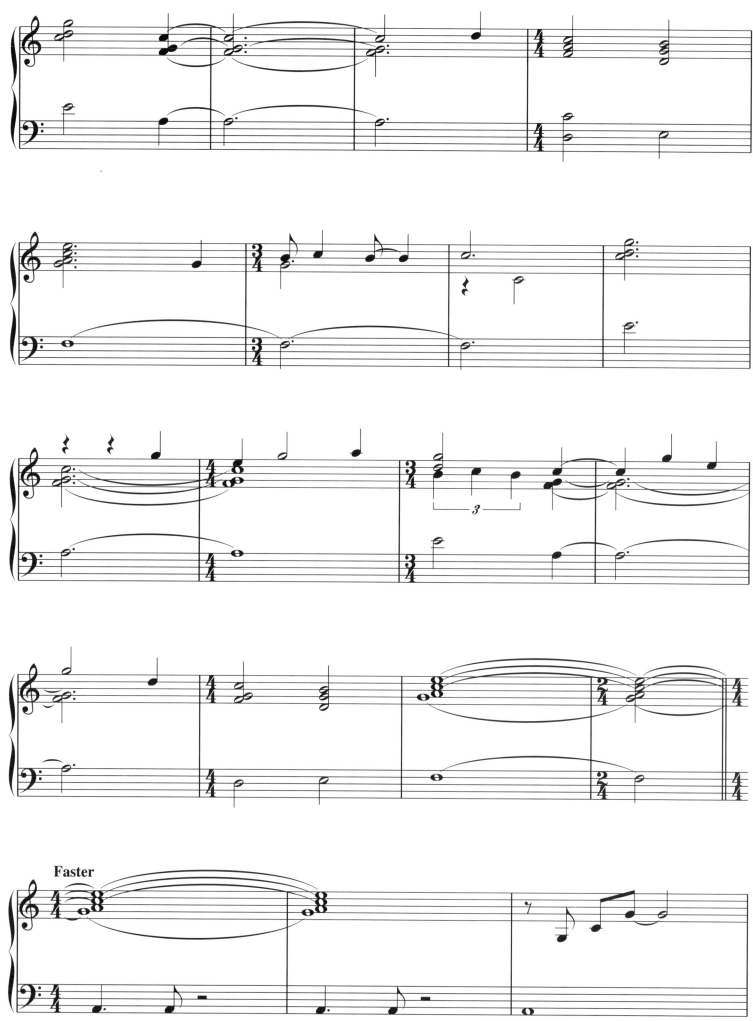

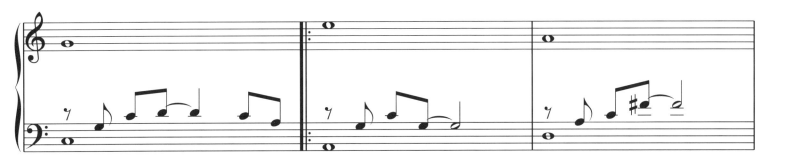

Repeat ad lib. and Fade

OCALA

Visitors to Florida are surprised to find that this state still has so much undeveloped land. The Ocala National Forest, which is close to the city where I live, is filled with sand pines, cypress and turkey oaks. Fortunately, these trees don't seem to interest the timber industry,

so they attract plenty of birds and wildlife instead. For people who live in large urban areas, it's reassuring to have wild, natural areas nearby. If you lose your perspective in the city, the best place to rediscover it is out here.

Artist portrait by Allan-Knox Studio

By WAYNE GRATZ

Brightly

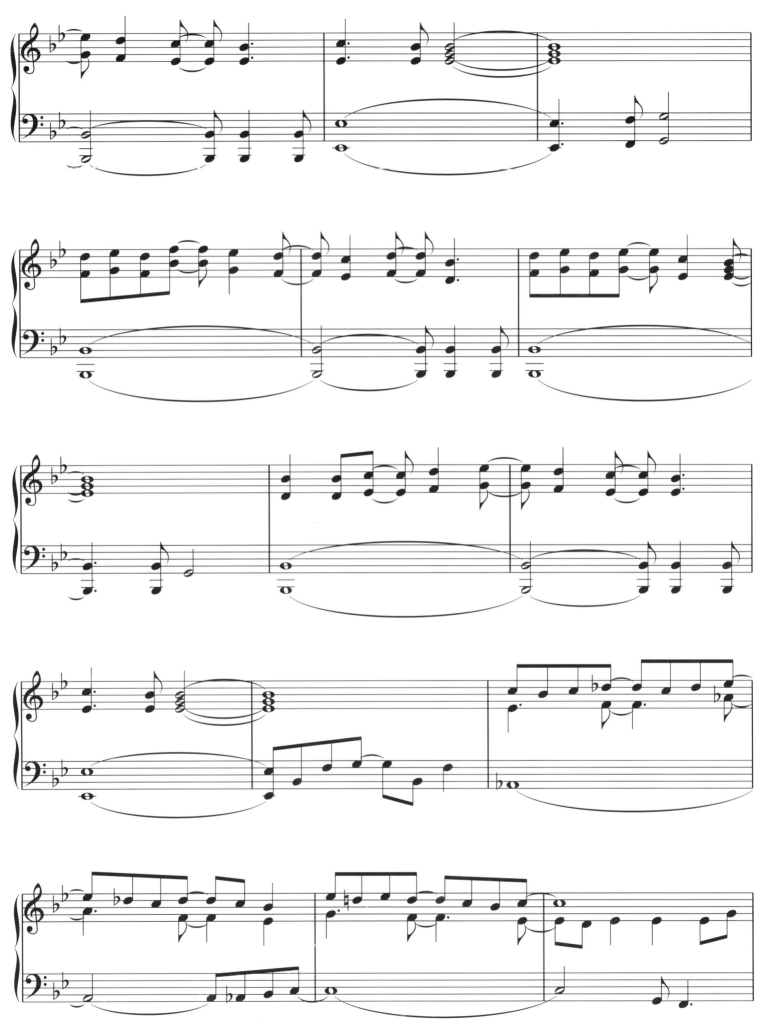

D.S. al Coda

CODA

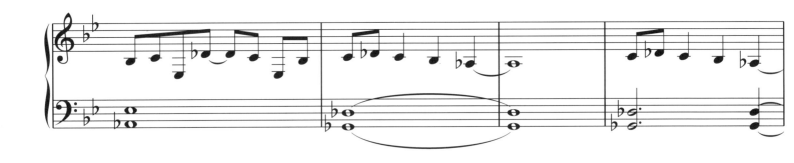

Repeat ad lib. and Fade

TAL

Tal is the Nepali word for lake. From the end of a jeep trail at Bhotehura, our party hiked for five days along the wild Marsyandi River, with the snow-capped Annapurnas towering above us. On the sixth day, we made a gruelling march up a narrow, zig-zagging trail etched into the canyon's sheer walls. After  hours of scrambling over rock slides and massive boulders, we stumbled into an unexpected, pristine valley. We celebrated by taking a bath in the lake — Tal.

Trapezoid

By PAUL REISLER
and BOB READ

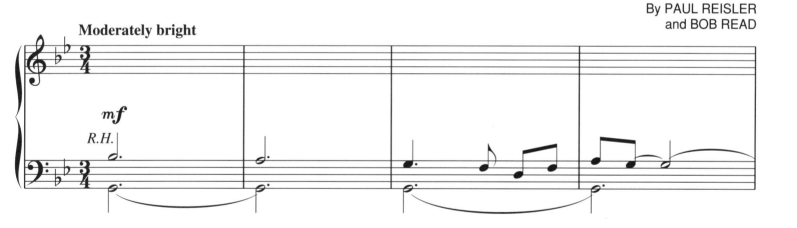

accel.

accel.

55

WHITE WATER

The only highways you will find in the wilderness are the rivers, full of free-flowing elegance and untamed power. The National Wild and Scenic Rivers System protects 120 U.S. river segments, but many other magnificent, beneficial rivers are threatened by various man-made intrusions: the Klamath in Oregon, by a proposed hydro-power diversion; the South Platte in Colorado and the American in California, by dams; the Bruneau/Jarbidge system in Idaho, by the expansion of an Air Force bombing range. Our rivers, like our rainforests and other natural treasures, need our care and concern.

Doug Cameron

Artist portrait by Karen Miller

By DOUG CAMERON

© 1990 Nara Music, Inc.
1845 North Farwell Avenue, Milwaukee, WI 53202

8va

Tempo 1

D.S. al Coda

CODA

3

3

Repeat and Fade

WILDFLOWERS

Each of us has a special place that offers us inspiration and renewal — the quiet waters of a secluded lake, a sunny glade deep in the forest, an alpine meadow bathed in cool, fresh mountain air. These are the gifts of the wilderness. As I sit at the piano, my imagination visits these places, and each one is filled with images of wildflowers. Whether they stand quietly in the forest or dance in the midday sun, their beauty commands my attention. As they open their petals to greet the day, I can almost hear their joyful cry: "I am!"

Artist portrait by V. Tony Hauser

By MICHAEL JONES

Moderately

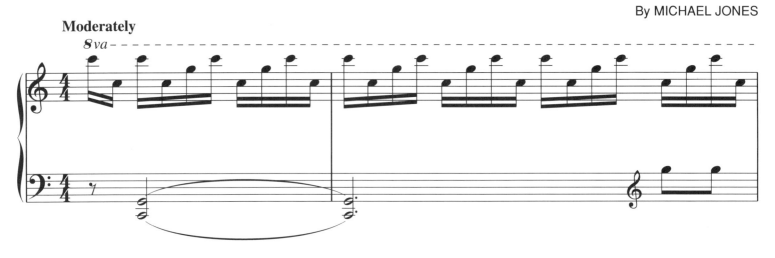

To Coda ⊕

rit.

rubato

rit.

ppp

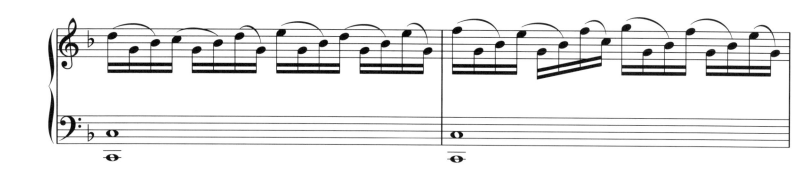

D.S. al Coda

CODA

Tempo 1

8va -

rit.

WONDERLAND

Maybe our schools should think about offering courses in phenology. Phenology is "observing and celebrating the gradual seasonal unfolding of natural wonders." Phenology means to me a rainbow of spring wildflowers dancing in the meadows, or a forest being slowly transformed by autumn's ritual of  *color. A walk in the wilderness is a visit to wonderland — a field trip in phenology. These wonder-lands allow us to discover peace and beauty in nature when we least expect it . . . and when we need it the most.*

By SPENCER BREWER

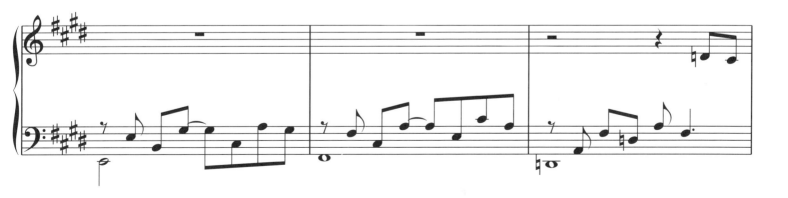

8va bassa

WOODLAND MISSION

Ancient forests once blanketed vast areas of North America, filling the horizons with towering, majestic trees. Today, it is estimated that only 10 to 15 percent of these virgin forests still stand, and that old-growth trees may vanish altogether by early in the next century. The trees that remain humble us with their magnificence and stead- fastness, yet their dwindling numbers also stir a compelling sense of urgency within those of us who stand in awe of their beauty.

Artist portrait by Richard Stefani

By WILLIAM ELLWOOD

Moderately bright

Repeat and Fade

NARADA LOTUS™
New Acoustic Music

N-61001	PIANOSCAPES	Michael Jones
N 61002	SEASONS	Gabriel Lee
N-61003	HEARTSOUNDS	David Lanz
N-61004	SEASCAPES	Michael Jones
N-61005	IMPRESSIONS	Gabriel Lee
N-61006	NIGHTFALL	David Lanz
N-61007	LOTUS SAMPLER #1	Narada Artists
N-61008	SOLSTICE	David Lanz and Michael Jones
N-61009	SUNSCAPES	Michael Jones
N-61010	OPENINGS	William Ellwood
N-61011	EMERALD	Brewer, Tingstad and Rumbel
N-61012	QUIET FIRE	Ancient Future
N-61013	LOTUS SAMPLER #2	Narada Artists
N-61014	AMBER	Michael Jones and David Darling
N-61015	RENAISSANCE	William Ellwood
N-61016	WOODLANDS	Tingstad, Rumbel and Lanz
N-61017	PORTRAITS	Spencer Brewer
N-61018	LOTUS SAMPLER #3	Narada Artists
N-61019	DEPARTURES	John Doan
N-61020	AFTER THE RAIN	Michael Jones
N-61021	CRISTOFORI'S DREAM	David Lanz
N-61022	LEGENDS	Eric Tingstad and Nancy Rumbel
N-61023	REMINISCENCE	Wayne Gratz
N-61024	VISTA	William Ellwood
N-61025	LOTUS SAMPLER #4	Narada Artists
N-61026	HOMELAND	Eric Tingstad and Nancy Rumbel
N-61027	MAGICAL CHILD	Michael Jones
N-61028	PANORAMA	Wayne Gratz
N-61029	WISDOM OF THE WOOD	Narada Artists
N-61030	MORNING IN MEDONTE	Michael Jones

NARADA MYSTIQUE™
New Electronic Music

N-62001	VALLEY IN THE CLOUDS	David Arkenstone
N-62002	THE WAITING	Peter Buffett
N-62003	HIDDEN PATHWAYS	Bruce Mitchell
N-62004	ONE BY ONE	Peter Buffett
N-62005	A VIEW FROM THE BRIDGE	Carol Nethen
N-62006	INTRUDING ON A SILENCE	Colin Chin
N-62007	DANCING ON THE EDGE	Bruce Mitchell
N-62008	CITIZEN OF TIME	David Arkenstone
N-62009	MYSTIQUE SAMPLER ONE	Narada Artists
N-62010	WARM SOUND IN	
N-62011	THE MESSENGE	
N-62012	LOST FRONTIE	
N-62013	YONNONDIO	

NARADA EQUII
New Age Fusion

N-63001	NATURAL ST	
N-63002	INDIAN SUMI	
N-63003	DESERT VISI	
N-63004	EQUINOX SA	

N-63005	ISLAND	David Arkenstone with Andrew White
N-63006	CIRCLE	Ralf Illenberger
N-63007	CROSS CURRENTS	Richard Souther
N-63008	DORIAN'S LEGACY	Spencer Brewer
N-63009	HEART & BEAT	Ralf Illenberger
N-63010	MIL AMORES	Doug Cameron
N-63011	MOON RUN	Trapezoid
N-63012	CAFÉ DU SOLEIL	Brian Mann
N-63013	WHITE LIGHT	Martin Kolbe
N-63014	NEW LAND	Bernardo Rubaja
N-63015	TWELVE TRIBES	Richard Souther
N-63016	EQUINOX SAMPLER TWO	Narada Artists
N-63017	AQUAMARINE	Friedemann
N-63018	THE PIPER'S RHYTHM	Spencer Brewer
N-63019	PLACES IN TIME	Michael Gettel
N-63020	JOURNEY TO YOU	Doug Cameron

NARADA COLLECTION SERIES™

N-39100	THE NARADA COLLECTION	Narada Artists
N-39117	THE NARADA COLLECTION TWO	Narada Artists
N-63902	THE NARADA CHRISTMAS COLLECTION	Narada Artists
N-63904	THE NARADA NUTCRACKER	Narada Artists
N-63905	THE NARADA WILDERNESS COLLECTION	Narada Artists
N-63906	THE NARADA COLLECTION THREE	Narada Artists
N-63907	A CHILDHOOD REMEMBERED	Narada Artists
N-63908	ALMA DEL SUR	Various Artists

NARADA ARTIST SERIES™

N-64001	SKYLINE FIREDANCE	David Lanz
N-64002	MICHAEL'S MUSIC	Michael Jones
N-64003	IN THE WAKE OF THE WIND	David Arkenstone
	RDEN	Eric Tingstad and bel
	THE HEART	David Lanz
	OF OLYMPIA	David Arkenstone th David Lanz

MA™

TRIBAL WISDOM AND	WORLD Hans Zimmer
AND THE AGE OF DISCOVERY	witz

*Narada appreciates the ... ...he music of our artists. Narada
publishes a free, semi-a... ...rtists as well as information on
new recordings. You may ... ...family of quality-minded listeners.
Please write to: Friends of ... ...of Narada, P.O. Box 2301, 1200
CH Hilversum, The Netherl...*

ML